ME THE PEOPLE

THE EDITORIAL CARTOONS
OF PIA GUERRA

Edited by Branwyn Bigglestone

Book Design by Drew Gill

IMAGE COMICS, INC. • Robert Kirkman: Chief Operating Officer • Erik Larsen: Chief Financial Officer • Todd McFarlane: President • Marc Silvestri: Chief Executive Officer • Jim Valentino: Vice President • Eric Stephenson: Publisher / Chief Creative Officer • Corey Hart: Director of Sales • Jeff Boison: Director of Publishing Planning & Book Trade Sales • Chris Ross: Director of Digital Sales • Jeff Stang: Director of Specialty Sales • Kat Salazar: Director of PR & Marketing • Drew Gill: Art Director • Heather Doornink: Production Director • Nicole Lapalme: Controller • IMAGECOMICS.COM

This book is dedicated to my mother, Leena, who didn't just tell me to do right, she DID right. Pictured here in 1971, getting ready to go to another anti-Vietnam War protest in Manhattan.

Also pictured—me, not quite ready to come out yet (which is why she wore the helmet—thanks, mom).

ACKNOWLEDGEMENTS

I would like to thank Justin Norman for doing what he has always done in the twenty plus years I've known him, and that's shoving me into the faces of editors despite all of my "I don't think I'm ready!" protestations. I've gotten so much work that way, and look, he's done it again by getting these cartoons in the face of Eric Stephenson and all the fine folks at Image Comics who were kind enough to take a chance on this project.

Dyane Hertogs for her advice and valuable overseas perspective.

Branwyn Bigglestone for all her amazing editorial work and hustle. Drew Gill for jumping on board as designer and art director.

Big thanks to Jamal Igle for taking the time to write from his heart.

Everyone at theNib.com for fighting the good fight and letting me ride shotgun.

To my sister Vicky Van who has always been my greatest cheerleader and never afraid to let me know when something sucks.

And so much gratitude to the love of my life, Ian Boothby. I wouldn't know how brutal these cartoons were if I didn't have your horrified cringes to let me know I'd nailed it.

INTRODUCTION

I'm not a happy person.

By nature, I suppose I'm the gregarious sort. I'm friendly, affable, surrounded by loving family and friends. That said, my happiness is being routinely pummeled like a contestant on a Japanese game show being hit with a kendo stick while dressed like a giant piece of onigiri.

Our world is under attack. It's not an attack that can be easily repelled. We're in the midst of an ideological war against an enemy that we created. An enemy we should be calling our brothers and sisters. This attack doesn't affect our borders but affects the world around us. We're being killed—physically and emotionally—with every school shooting, every story of women being abused by men in positions of power, by every moment of casual racism becoming blatant and aggressive. We're worked to the point of illness and death with no relief, the high cost of basic healthcare destroying lives. Corporations poison our water, then overcharge us for those basic things we need most. Through outdated methodology, a known huckster was placed at head of the United States of America. In the almost two years since the 2016 elections, we've seen our civil discourse carved away, and our most basic principles eroded by a simple change in ideology. We've seen the rise of autocratic politicians and the return of a type of fascism we swore we would never allow to return. Where the very concepts of "Life, Liberty and The Pursuit of Happiness" are constantly questioned by those in power.

When bombarded by the constant onslaught of horrible news, it's difficult not to feel like a block of cheddar cheese being tossed into a wood chipper. It's overkill and only gets messier from there. We need to find our happiness, we need to laugh at the absurdity we're surrounded by.

As a fan of Pia Guerra's beautiful comic art, the work presented in this collection has become one of the salves in my daily life. It's not just well drawn, which would be a selling point to me on its own. Pia's comedic point of view is strikingly accurate. It's voicing the feelings of a lot of us, yet with a sense of humor reminiscent of political satirists like Tom Lehrer, Jon Stewart, and David Frost. It's sharp, biting, and tempered by gorgeous linework created by a master draftsperson. Pia makes me laugh, and as a person who swims along the edge of the pool in the political world, she helps me in my search for happiness in the outside world.

Jamal Igle

Jamal Yaseem Igle is an American comic book artist, editor, art director, marketing executive and animation storyboard artist. The creator of the comic book series *Molly Danger,* he is also known for his pencilling, inking and coloring work on books such as *Supergirl* and *Firestorm*.

We were at an election night party at our friends David and Alison's house in Vancouver. It was supposed to be a fun night of poker, CNN commentary, and homemade cookies in the shape of Captain America's shield—a tradition that had started with President Obama's win in 2008 and later, Prime Minister Justin Trudeau's in 2015. Added to birthdays, New Years, and Oscar Night (where David and Alison's own Oscar for Best Animated Short of 1994 would be proudly on display), these get-togethers were just a good excuse for a gaggle of reclusive creative types to get out of their respective studios and pretend we were still able to socialize like honest-to-goodness, real life folks.

Despite all the nervousness, we were hopeful. The overall consensus among experts was that it would be close, but a handful of key states would very likely block a Trump electoral win—that it would take something extraordinary to turn them all red... So yeah, hopeful.

Returns started coming as the guests did, each new arrival asking to confirm the latest numbers, not sure if what they had heard on their car radios was right. The mood began to steadily darken. So much red creep. We could not stop watching it, and the poker game never got going.

Surely the next state would block a Trump win. Or the next one. Come on, really?

And then Alison summed up that sick, sinking feeling of watching the unfolding of a horror: "It feels like 9/11."

I wanted to deny that comparison—everyone in the room did—but really, we couldn't. We all got quiet and the realization hit hard: this was happening. The biggest joke of a human being in the world was going to be President.

It wasn't that we were so naive as to think that it was outside of the realm of possibility. We saw the rallies, heard the dangerous rhetoric. We remembered how Palin brought out that ferocious, dark side of American consciousness four years earlier. But we also saw every single paper of record endorse the more qualified candidate. We saw the debates where Clinton clearly trounced this idiotic, bigoted P.T. Barnum who had nothing, no platform of substance, who stirred up a frenzy of racism and misogyny, who lied and lied and lied.

There were more people out there who would stand up to this, just as they did with Palin, right? Technically, as we'd soon learn, nearly three million more, but it wasn't enough.

I remember waking up the morning after the election, from the pleasant disassociation of sleep, to one of the most awake moments I've ever experienced. I was overwhelmed with disgust, disappointment, sadness, and the kind of anxiety for the future I haven't felt since I was a kid after seeing the anti-nuclear war documentary, *If You Love This Planet.* A feeling that crumbled along with the Berlin Wall and then the USSR, taking all its nuclear-fueled nightmares with it.

But here it was again—a shiny new sledge hammer of grossness that just kept slamming away with every thought of that snide, bullying smirk. You can't feel this and not want to do something, anything, if only to feel you're not doing nothing.

So I picked up a pencil and started to draw.

SMH.
November 9th, 2016

DAY 1

Day One.
October 24th, 2016

Mirror.
January 8th, 2016

Repellant.
January 7th, 2016

Throne.
December 16th, 2016

Liar Liar.
January 19th, 2016

He's Such a Smart Boy.
January 6th, 2017

HEY NEWS AGENCIES! CAN'T FIND A COURT ARTIST
FOR THE NEXT CLOSED WHITE HOUSE PRESS CONFERENCE?
TRY THESE PRE-DRAWN SKETCHES!

TAKING QUESTIONS.

UH-OH, A TOUGH ONE
FROM APRIL.

DEER IN THE HEADLIGHTS.

"HE TWEETED WHAT?"

"OH GOD, WHY ME?"

"I CAN'T TAKE IT
ANYMORE!"

Spiced Up.
June 22nd, 2017

Big Boy.
January 30th, 2017

U.S. Customs and Border Protection

Banned.
January 30th, 2017

Douglass.
February 1st, 2017

"BAD DUDE"

"Bad Dude."
February 7th, 2017

Murrow.
February 5th, 2017

Golden Years.
February 14th, 2017

Sweet Dreams.
February 4th, 2017

Puzzled.
February 14th, 2017

Circus.
February 12th, 2017

Mike's Turn.
February 16th, 2017

Float.
March 23rd, 2017

SUMMER HAS COME EARLY FOR THE
WASHINGTON PRESS CORPS.

Leaky.
February 13th, 2017

Wipeout.
February 18th, 2017

Dance.
February 26th, 2017

Kislyak.
March 6th, 2017

Me Me Me.
April 28th, 2017

Sucker.
March 10th, 2017

Meanwhile, in Canada...
June 5th, 2017

You Shall Not Pass.
May 5th, 2017

Shake, Rattle and Roll.
May 15th, 2017

Homecoming.
May 26th, 2017

Dominoes.
May 22nd, 2017

Bedtime for Bozo.
May 26th, 2017

Nice'n Easy.
April 15th, 2017

"LOOK FOR THE HELPERS."

Manchester.
May 21st, 2017

Make My Life Great Again.
April 25th, 2017

100 Digs.
April 23rd, 2017

I AM TRUMP.
May 8th, 2017

"Tapes."
May 12th, 2017

Electoral Dysfunction.
February 22nd, 2017

RECONSTRUCTION   DECONSTRUCTION

Ashes to Ashes.
February 23rd, 2017

Dark Elf.
June 8th, 2017

"Bad Hombres."
February 23rd, 2017

Aw Nuts!
April, 2017

Unknown.
January 7th, 2016

AW NUTS!
WELL! HERE COMES OL' JARED KUSHNER!
GOOD OL' JARED KUSHNER...YES, SIR!

Aw Nuts!
May 28th, 2017

Comey Testimony.
June 8th, 2017

WELCOME TO THE MIDDLE OF THE BOOK!
AND NOW A WORD FROM THE EDITOR...

The opposition bombards us with "Pull yourself up by your bootstraps!" because they're hoping we won't notice through all that noise that not all bootstraps are created equal.

If the Big Bad Wolf blows your house down, you want version 2.0 of your home to incorporate more advanced materials and engineering so that jerk can't blow it down again. But there's always a guy yelling at you to quit dwelling on the past and blaming others for you being a homeless bum, and that guy is the Big Bad Wolf. Why would you listen to him?

Sadly, many do. And that gives Big Bad the space and opportunity to rewrite history, letting him convince everyone that the house wanted to be blown down, if it was even blown down, which it wasn't, it just fell down because you built it wrong in the first place! So stop blaming the poor, innocent Wolf for all your problems!

Actually, I'm feeling bad about using an endangered species to make my point, so I'm going to switch gears to what are, amazingly, real-life examples:

In 2010, Arizona House Bill 2281 was signed into law banning ethnic studies out of fear that students might find out that some white people and policies in American history were maybe a little bit racist, and then try to overthrow the government.

Textbooks adopted by the Texas State Board of Education end up being ordered by school districts all over the country, giving those Texans who wish to spread disinformation the opportunity to seed the future of the country with lies. For example, these books have claimed things like Moses was basically a Founding Father, African slaves were "workers" who "immigrated" to the colonies, and that the Civil War was totally about some other stuff that definitely wasn't slavery.

Speaking of the Civil War, how about those Confederate monuments? Torch-wielding "very fine people" felt so strongly about "protecting history" that they physically assaulted several people and murdered a woman. But it's never been about protecting history, it's about protecting an image. Monuments lack context unto themselves, and if all of the statues erected are of white men, the message is clear: there is nobody else of historical consequence. These dudes are the ones who matter.

Oh, and from Day 1, the Trump administration has been scrubbing government websites of any inconvenient information that doesn't jibe with his brand of America™.

So what do we do? What can we do? Oh gosh, there's so much! For starters...

SHUT UP AND LISTEN! Listen for what's being said and for what's not being said. Take note of which reporters ask follow-up questions. Bookmark the dog whistles. Do the words match reality? Consider the source. Who does the speaker associate with? What does their body language say? Please don't just put on an "ERACISM" shirt and leave it at that. Listen to those without power and privilege. Engage those who you seek to help. Don't just impose your idea of progress and wait for the accolades to roll in.

SPEAK UP AND DEMAND TO BE HEARD! There is so much bullshit that needs calling out. Some methods are more effective than others, different situations call for different approaches, and sometimes it's just not safe. You need to find your voice when and where you can. Use whatever power and privilege you may have to help others to find theirs, and amplify the righteous. Point a giant neon sign at all forms of voter suppression. If you ask, "Why is this company allowed to poison us?" and the answer is, "America is the best, freedom eagles soar in heaven with Jesus, and my party is the only one fighting to keep America strong and free, the end," spit hellfire back at them. Because that's just snake oil.

QUESTION YOUR OWN DEFAULT SETTINGS! We all have our own set of assumptions and prejudices, born of a combination of nature, nurture, and cognitive shortcuts. Nobody is entirely free of confirmation bias, groupthink, the bandwagon effect, clustering illusion, or even of just being off your game on a given day. The process of self-reflection, recognition, and correction must be ongoing.

VOTE IN EVERY SINGLE ELECTION! It's going to take all of us, using whatever particular skills and knowledge we can bring to the table, to fight the new stealth tech Jim Crow and political disfranchisement. Yes, think globally, but act locally. The enormity of the problem can feel crushing, so find a local nonprofit that speaks to you, and support them in whatever functional capacity you can.

Now...

FINISH READING THE SECOND HALF OF THIS BOOK, AND LET'S GET TO WORK!

Branwyn Bigglestone
July 2018

IVANKA TRUMP

Jackboot Collection

AVAILABLE AT TRUMP TOWERS ISTANBUL

Footwear.
May 1st, 2017

IVANKA TRUMP

Jackboot Collection

AVAILABLE AT TRUMP TOWERS ISTANBUL

Clubbing.
April 18th, 2017

Flash.
June 26th, 2017

Safe.
June 10th, 2017

Lame.
June 27th, 2017

Red Flag.
June 29th, 2017

The Ever Changing Story.
July 11th, 2017

Lazy.
August 2nd, 2017

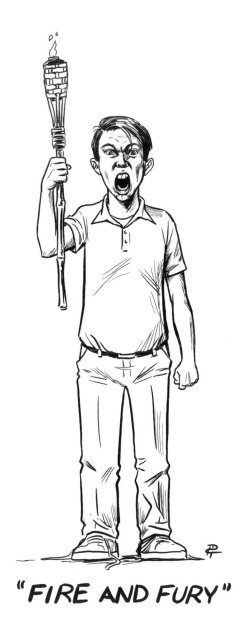

"FIRE AND FURY"

Alt Blight.
August 5th, 2017

Shoe.
August 22nd, 2017

Broflake.
August 15th, 2017

BUT WHAT DO WE REPLACE THEM WITH?

Monuments.
August 17th, 2017

Take a Knee.
September 24th, 2017

Spent.
July 29th, 2017

All Wet.
August 26th, 2017

Blindsided.
October 8th, 2017

HE'S MAKING A LIST, HE'S CHECKING IT TWICE...

Naughty List.
November 18th, 2017

Here's Robbie!
October 21st, 2017

POS.
September 27th, 2017

Vote.
October 30th, 2017

Low.
January 6th, 2018

Wake Up.
January 11th, 2018

TRUMP MARKS FIRST ANNIVERSARY
OF HIS SWEARING IN.

Happy Anniversary.
January 18th, 2018

Number One Fan.
January 3rd, 2018

Lights Out.
January 21st, 2018

Emperor's New Robe.
January 22nd, 2018

Gate.
February 15th, 2018

Hero's Welcome.
February 15th, 2018

2004.
February 16th, 2018

Emma.
February 19th, 2018

Diptych.
February 18th, 2018

Cell Phone.
March 30th, 2018

Draylen Mason.
March 4th, 2018

Bedtime Story.
March 17th, 2018

Damascus.
April 2nd, 2018

Glass Ceiling.
May 10th, 2018

FLICKED.
April 27th, 2018

Playground.
May 17th, 2018

Cage.
May 20th, 2018

Snatcher.
June 19th, 2018

Daddy's Home.
June 14th, 2018

Cover Girl.
June 21st, 2018

Me Me Me Time.
June 21st, 2018

War Zone.
June 29th, 2018

Breaking News.
June 29th, 2018

But Doctor...
June 6th, 2018

The Art of the Hostage Negotiation.
June 19th, 2018

The Wheels on the Baby Prison Bus Go Round and Round.
June 4th, 2018

Reunited.
July 9th, 2018

Based on a True Story.
June 23rd, 2018

AND HERE WE ARE...

Looking at what's been happening since that escalator ride in 2015, it seems so very familiar. This constant, day-to-day shit show that never ends, crisis upon crisis, inflammatory tweets, racist dog whistles, and one legal battle after the next. I'm writing this in July 2018, and the mid-terms are just a few months away. He's presently en route to meet with Vladimir Putin after making a shambles of NATO and pissing off pretty much everyone in the UK. He started at the top of the escalator, and it's been all downhill from there.

It's this current world tour of bigotry and stupidity that has me thinking about Blitzkrieg.

Blitzkrieg was a form of warfare used by the Nazis to overwhelm, unbalance, and demoralize. Attack fast, relentlessly from all sides, by land, air, and sea, using advanced technology until the enemy submits.

Lean back a bit and you may see that this new steady doling out of outrageous acts resembles a modern form of Blitzkrieg. The territory now is psychological, the weapons are digital, spreading misinformation, conflicting standards, proclamations, executive orders, straight up lies.

The more ridiculous of these end up being labeled "distractions," but they're all part of the same strategy, not meant to make you look the other way, but to tire you from looking at all, to make you turn away in disgust from all the input. They keep throwing noodles on the wall to see not just what sticks, but to make you not want to be in the kitchen anymore because there's just no way to clean up the mess.

It's far from sophisticated, but you don't need sophistication to impress the unsophisticated. Namely, his base of the uneducated, the greedy, the brutal, all looking for any validation they can find to justify the cruelty that sits in their hearts; to have one over on the ones they've been convinced are keeping them down.

In the face of all this senselessness, this continual corruption of norms that every day is described as "unprecedented" instead of what it really is – batshit crazy – how do you as a citizen respond when it seems like no one is being held accountable? When those who call for responsibility are demonized. When those calling out racists are themselves called bigots? Again, it makes you want to just leave the kitchen. Maybe if we wait this will all blow over. After the next election.

But it's not just about voting. Yes, by good God you must vote, but you also have to change minds. You have to confront those who don't see their vote as consequential and have abstained, those who voted for this madness thinking it would shake things up, and those who believed in the false equivalency that both parties are just as bad. These are toxic ideas that benefit tyrants and have to be put down. These are people who, in many cases, want to take away your vote. Don't do their job for them.

There are so many obstacles in place, especially for marginalized communities: voter suppression, reduction in polling stations, limited hours, pulled registrations, deliberate misinformation, all designed to keep voters away. If you see this happening in your districts, you must speak up. If you have even a little privilege, you must use it. Contact your representatives, leave messages, politely pester them to act. Politicians have to keep track of their calls, to gauge responses, and the more they get, the more they'll listen. It doesn't have to be elaborate, just a call saying, "I'm a constituent, this is a problem, and I want you to act on it." A minute out of your day can have a lot of weight.

The Blitzkrieg of batshit and bigotry is not unstoppable. One only has to look to the UK and how they stood their ground against the world crashing in around them to see that it's possible to do so against this psychological onslaught.

Your greatest weapon is the truth; spread it around and don't feel any obligation to engage with disingenuous demands on your time. Block anyone who tries to argue in bad faith, leave your truth and carry on. Find your touchstones, your Patronuses, your sacred objects, whether it's Captain Rogers' shield or Mr. Rogers' smile, let them keep you focused.

Hate and despair will eat you alive.

Your armour is resolve, kindness, creativity, and humour. These will get you through the night. Authoritarians can't connect to any of these. They have no patience, no empathy, absolutely no ability to create anything of their own, and are total shit at comedy because its job is to point out hypocrisy and lies. That's your advantage. Find the thing you're good at. Everybody has one – a craft, a skill, a weird party trick – use it to share your thoughts. If you can embroider, do up some subversive cross-stitch. If you can bake, make some funny cookies. If you can draw (hello!), do up some cartoons. Write an essay, a savage haiku, make a meme. Get it online and share it!

Find your allies, support one another, maintain morale, and resist. It's a long-term fight, so you have to pace yourself. Take breaks when you need it, come back into the fray when fresh.

But most of all, laugh. Laugh while you're doing these things, laugh at these basic, cruel assholes because it drives them crazy. Mockery makes it harder for the normalization to find solid ground. Keep it off balance. Keep knocking it back. Resist.

Happy hunting.

Pia Guerra
July 2018

Pia Guerra is a Vancouver-based cartoonist who was co-creator and lead penciller of the award-winning comic book *Y: The Last Man* with writer Brian K. Vaughan and inker Jose Marzan Jr.

Following the 2016 election, Pia started drawing editorial cartoons using her art to speak out against the racism and misogyny she saw in the Trump administration.

Shortly after the inauguration, her cartoon *Big Boy* went viral, appearing on several news outlets including CNN and ABC's *Good Morning America*. This led to being asked to be a regular contributor to the editorial cartoons website www.theNib.com.

Pia is married to writer Ian Boothby who she collaborates with on many projects, including creating cartoons for *The New Yorker Magazine*.